ONE
TIMES
SQUARE

A Century of Change
at the Crossroads
of the World

ONE

A Century of Change at

TIMES

the Crossroads of the World

SQUARE

written & illustrated by

JOE McKENDRY

DAVID R. GODINE
Publisher · Boston

For Mom and Dad

First published in 2012 by
DAVID R. GODINE · *Publisher*
Post Office Box 450
Jaffrey, New Hampshire 03452
www.godine.com

LIBRARY OF CONGRESS CATALOGING-IN-PUBLICATION DATA

McKendry, Joe, 1972–
One Times Square : a century of change at the crossroads of the world /
written and illustrated by Joe McKendry.
    p. cm.
Includes bibliographical references.
ISBN-13: 978-1-56792-364-3 (alk. paper)
ISBN-10: 1-56792-364-X
1. Times Square (New York, N.Y.)—History—Juvenile literature.
2. New York (N.Y.)—History—Juvenile literature. I. Title.
F128.65.T5M37 2012
974.7'1—dc23
2011027379

FIRST EDITION
Printed in China

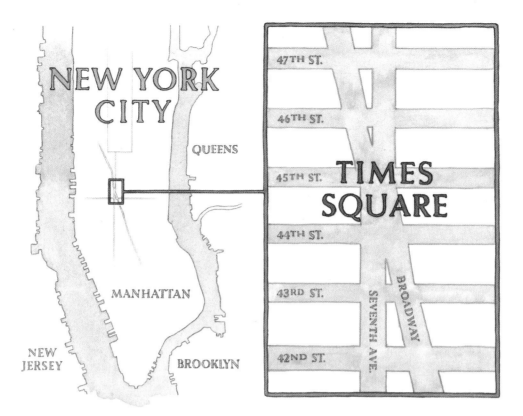

At the heart of New York City lies the junction of Seventh Avenue and Broadway, perhaps the most well known intersection in the world. Every year, Times Square attracts roughly one million people to its famous New Year's Eve celebration, while an estimated 200 million tune in from home as the lighted ball makes its descent atop One Times Square.

What transformed this once humble carriage district into "The Crossroads of the World"? From its earliest days, entertainment, up-to-the-minute information, and public celebrations have defined Times Square, almost instantaneously establishing it as the nerve center of the city whose influence reaches around the globe. Over more than a century, Times Square has never stopped evolving, representing highly different extremes of American culture from glamour to squalor.

Through all of the changes, One Times Square – the only surviving building from Times Square's beginning in 1904 – has stood faithful as the keeper of time, marking each passing year with the annual New Year's ball drop. Like the rest of the square, its appearance has evolved, but the slender tower on 42nd Street continues to keep watch over a place that has undergone changes as dramatic as any place on earth.

Today's Times Square sits on land once owned by Medcef Eden, a brewer-turned-farmer whose seventy-acre farm covered much of the area in the early 1800s. Broadway was a dirt path known as Bloomingdale Road, rolling through a rural landscape of shantytowns and grazing cows. By the 1870s the city's population reached one million (up from just 60,000 in 1800), and construction of new homes and businesses was surging steadily northward along the strict grid that city surveyors laid out for Manhattan in 1811.

Carriage builders, livery stables, and a few coal yards moved into the intersection of Broadway and Seventh Avenue, earning it the nickname "Long Acre Square" after a carriage district in London. By night, the pickpockets who frequented the nearby brothels coined a less flattering name: "The Thieves' Lair."

Carriage builders, livery stables, and a few coal yards moved into the intersection of Broadway and Seventh Avenue, earning it the nickname "Long Acre Square" after a carriage district in London. By night, the pickpockets who frequented the nearby brothels coined a less flattering name: "The Thieves' Lair."

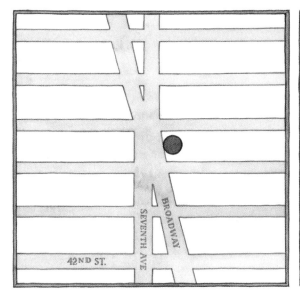
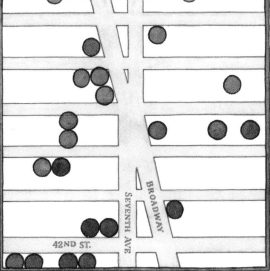

1899   **1915**

Theaters in Times Square

Among the first entrepreneurs to envision a more glamorous future for Long Acre Square was Oscar Hammerstein. The flamboyant theater impresario (and grandfather of the famed songwriter of the same name) built two major theaters there, the Olympia in 1895 and the Victoria in 1899. Despite the neighborhood's sketchy reputation, other theater owners followed and would soon create a new theater district for New York, adding new lights to Broadway's "Great White Way."

Hammerstein's larger-than-life personality was reflected in the Victoria Theatre's Roof Garden, which hosted performances during the summer when the main theater was too hot. The open-air space featured a promenade and an outdoor café and was later expanded to the roof of Hammerstein's Republic Theater, where the showman installed a "Dutch farm" complete with live cows, a duck pond, and a windmill. Novelty acts like boxing baboons, wrestling ponies, and stunt bicyclists shared the bill with big-name performers like Harry Houdini, regularly drawing standing-room-only crowds to the 600-seat theater.

The year 1904 brought dramatic changes to Long Acre Square, among them the completion of the Astor Hotel (A), New York's first subway (B), and – most notably – the new headquarters for the *New York Times* (C), whose imposing presence inspired a new name for the square. On April 19, 1904 Mayor George B. McClellan Jr. signed a proposal that officially renamed "the intersection of Broadway and Seventh Avenue bounded by 42nd and 47th Streets" as Times Square. Covering the event in its own pages, the *Times* crowed, "It is a name . . . not likely to be forgotten in this community."

1904

The *Times'* headquarters building, known as the Times Tower, was an impressive twenty-five-story structure modeled after Giotto's campanile for the cathedral in Florence, Italy. Ornate limestone, terra cotta, and brick encased what its builders boasted was "the stiffest steel frame of similar dimensions ever constructed." Equally impressive was its underground structure, which reached a full five stories below ground to accommodate both the subway and the newspaper's presses. Including the basement level, it was the tallest building in the world upon its completion – second tallest (after the Park Row Building in New York) in its official above-ground measurement of 395 feet.

On the building's first-ever New Year's Eve, the *Times* hosted an all-day street festival culminating in a dramatic fireworks display launched from the roof of the Times Tower. The celebration was so successful that Times Square quickly replaced Trinity Church (whose bells traditionally "rang in" the New Year) as New York's symbol of New Year's Eve. When the fireworks display was banned two years later, *New York Times* owner Adolph Ochs was forced to create a new tradition. "Time balls" like the ones mounted in Greenwich, England, and other coastal cities, which dropped at a specified time so that sailors could accurately set their chronometers, inspired Ochs. He commissioned the construction of a lighted sphere that could be lowered from the tower's 77-foot flagpole to mark the New Year. Constructed of wood and iron, the ball measured 5 feet in diameter, weighed 700 pounds, and contained 100 25-watt bulbs.

An early roadblock to the construction of the Times Tower was posed by Charles Thorley, a wealthy and self-important florist who owned a plot of land on the site of the proposed skyscraper. He reluctantly agreed to sell his land on the condition that his name be engraved on the new building. The Times obliged, placing a plaque so far above the sidewalk that only passing pigeons could see it.

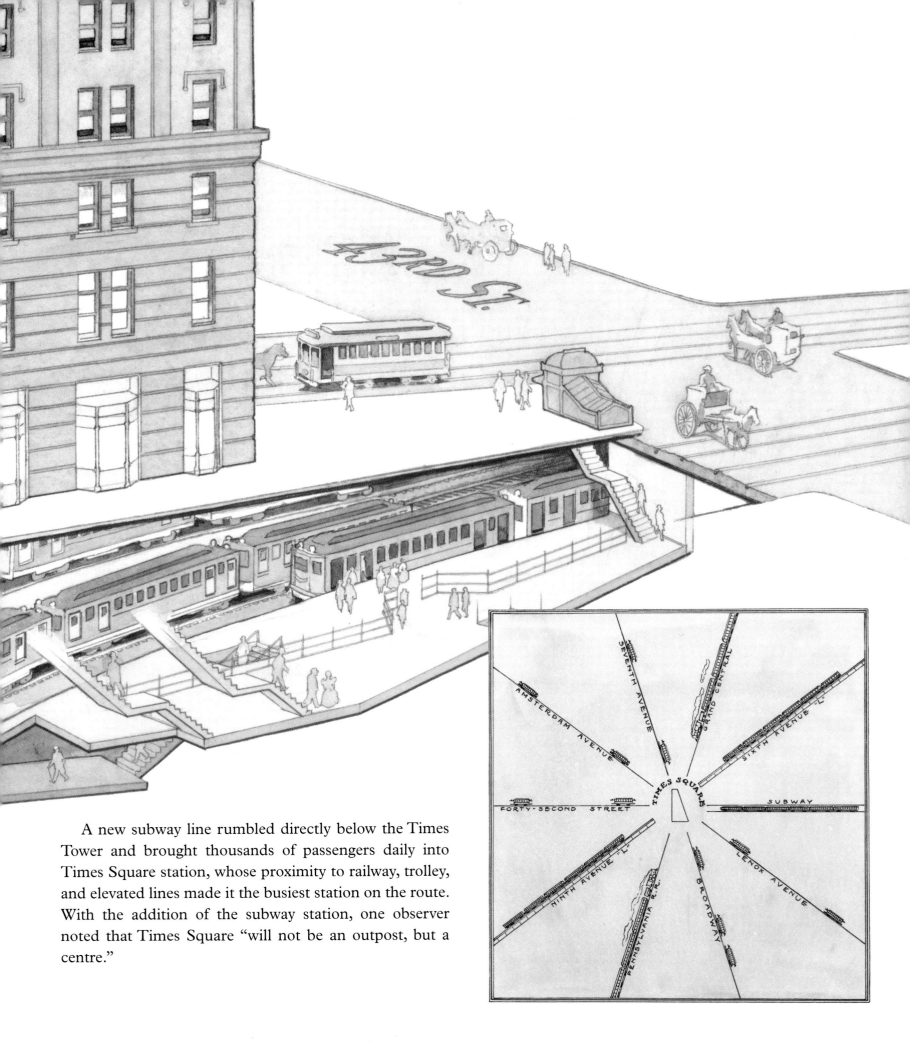

A new subway line rumbled directly below the Times Tower and brought thousands of passengers daily into Times Square station, whose proximity to railway, trolley, and elevated lines made it the busiest station on the route. With the addition of the subway station, one observer noted that Times Square "will not be an outpost, but a centre."

Always searching for opportunities to capture the attention of the square's visitors, *Times* owner Adolph Ochs developed inventive ways to generate crowds – and publicity – outside his newspaper headquarters. During the 1912 Presidential election, images were projected from a temporary shed built over the subway kiosk onto a screen mounted on the northern side of the tower, displaying pictures of the candidates, cartoons, and tally results to a crowd of more than 100,000. A searchlight mounted on top of the tower, which would announce the president by pointing in a specified direction, brought cheers (and jeers) when its northerly beam indicated the victory of Woodrow Wilson. Boxing matches, early milestones in aviation, and world events drew large crowds to informative displays on the tower. For World Series baseball games, a "Play-O-Graph" board mounted on the north façade of the building allowed crowds to "watch" the game in real time. As its operators followed the action by wire or telephone, they re-enacted the plays by moving pieces that showed the trajectory of hits and the movements of players. Ochs's determined efforts to bolster the reputation and readership of his newspaper resulted in its outgrowing the narrow Times Tower in 1913. Though the paper moved its operations to 43rd Street that year, the company retained ownership of the Tower and used a small portion of the building to house its classified advertising department.

Also intent on capturing the attention of Times Square's visitors were the advertisers, who coveted the open expanse of the bowtie-shaped square and the blocks-long visibility it could provide for their billboards. In 1917, Wrigley's Gum mounted the square's first truly massive billboard. The block-long sign on the Putnam building between 43rd and 44th streets along Seventh Avenue featured colorful peacocks, fountains, and animated "spearmen" who performed a "daily dozen" series of exercises.

In the 1920s, the fast-growing motion picture industry brought radical changes to Times Square. Loew's State Theatre (A) and its adjoining office building, which became Loew's headquarters, hosted world premieres of many of its films. Not to be outdone, Paramount Studios (B) began construction of its worldwide headquarters and an ornate flagship theater, demolishing an entire city block (including the former Putnam Building, onetime home of the Wrigley's "spearmen") to gain a prestigious Times Square address.

To accommodate the increasing number of weary tourists who came to enjoy the area's entertainment venues, more hotels sprang up, including the 700-room Hotel Claridge (C).

1926

HOTEL CLARIDGE
BEAU GESTE
HERBERT BRENON'S
BEAU GESTE
CRITERION
44TH ST. HOTEL CLARIDGE
44TH ST.
SQUIBB'S
DENTAL

Upon its completion in 1926 and at thirty-three stories, the Paramount Building became the tallest building in Times Square and would remain so for nearly fifty years. Its imposing 3,600-seat Paramount Theatre, with frescoed and gilt ceilings and grand lobby, set a new standard for the "movie palaces" popular in the decade leading up to the Great Depression. The opulent theaters of this period would soon be relics of the past as the country was struck with its worst financial crisis to date.

The Stock Market crash of October 29, 1929, which triggered the Great Depression, hit the city hard, and the bad news traveled fast thanks to telegraphs and radio. News of the worsening crisis on Wall Street flashed to anxious crowds in Times Square via the recently installed "Zipper" sign.

The Motograph News Bulletin, better known as the "Zipper," began broadcasting up-to-the-minute news on a five-foot-high electronic panel in 1928. A marvel of its time, it wrapped 360 feet around the Times Tower, consisted of 14,800 amber bulbs, 1,386,000 feet of wire, and more solder connections than all of the billboards in Times Square combined. As news bulletins were phoned in from the *New York Times* headquarters, the words were spelled out, letter by letter, by workers in the tower. Each letter was represented by a $7\frac{1}{2}'' \times 3''$ metal plate with the shape of the letter slightly raised above the surface (A). The plates were laid facedown on a frame that rode along a moving belt above a field of electrified brushes (B) that made contact with the raised letters as they passed along, opening and closing electrical circuits connected by wires to the corresponding field of bulbs on the face of the building (C). As the plates moved from brush to brush, the bulbs were switched on and off in rapid sequence, and the words appeared to travel around the building.

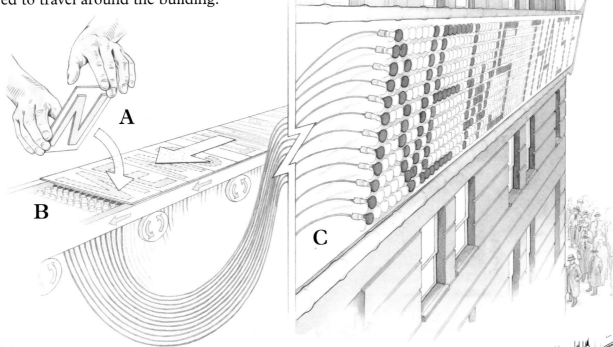

A

B

C

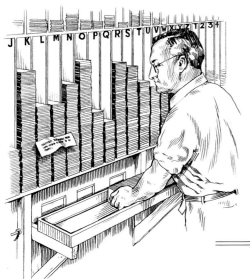

James Torpey was one of three operators responsible for setting bulletins for the "Zipper" from the control room on the fourth floor of One Times Square. He inaugurated the sign by laying out the message announcing Herbert Hoover's victory over Al Smith in the 1928 presidential election and spent the next thirty-three years announcing breaking news stories (often before they were broadcast on the radio) from baseball scores, to the Stock Market crash, to the end of the Second World War.

The depression brought new building construction in the area to a standstill, but it failed to make a lasting dent in the sign industry, which continued to produce the enormous billboards – or "spectaculars" as they were commonly known – that had come to define the look of Times Square.

In 1936, Wrigley's Gum mounted another block-long spectacular, advertised as "The Brightest Spot along the Great White Way." Built on the roof of the two-story International Casino, the Wrigley "aquarium" featured brightly colored fish whose animated lights created the illusion that they were swimming. The completed sign contained 29,508 light receptacles, 1,084 feet of neon tubing, and 70 miles of insulated wire. To change burnt-out bulbs, workers dangled high above street level using a block and tackle attached to a trolley rail that allowed them to move anywhere on the sign.

With the onset of the Second World War, Times Square's iconic billboards went dark. Lighting restrictions designed to prevent easy enemy targeting went into effect citywide. But a new icon – a replica of the Statue of Liberty – emerged as a constant reminder of the freedom Americans were struggling to preserve. Erected on the small island just in front of One Times Square, the statue was also a promotion for the sale of War Bonds, which could be purchased on site. An outdoor stage just below the statue hosted lunchtime performances by stars like bandleader Artie Shaw to draw attention to the cause.

Soldiers and sailors flocked to Times Square to enjoy the area's entertainment venues before shipping out. The Stage Door Canteen on 44th Street treated members of the military to free shows and offered patrons a chance to mingle or even dance with major Broadway and Hollywood stars. Thanks to high levels of foot traffic, the recruiting station at Times Square was among the most successful in the country, not only for men but also for women, who could sign up for the Women's Army Auxiliary Corps at a booth on the small triangle of open space just north of 46th Street, a spot known as Duffy Square.

The plot of land between Seventh Avenue and Broadway running from 45th to 47th Street is called Duffy Square. Dedicated in 1937 by Mayor Fiorello H. La Guardia and marked with a monument, the spot honors Father Francis P. Duffy, a Catholic priest who served as a military chaplain during the First World War and became the most highly decorated cleric in the history of the U.S. Army.

After years of war, the announcement on August 14, 1945, of an armistice with Japan was cause for celebration. An estimated 750,000 people flooded Times Square to join the largest spontaneous celebration the square had seen to date (A). Strangers hugged and kissed as the announcement flashed across the Zipper: "★★★OFFICIAL – TRUMAN ANNOUNCES JAPANESE SURRENDER★★★" The ball drop, suspended for two years during the war under citywide dim-out restrictions, could resume its lighted descent once again (B) and in the following decade would mark the fiftieth anniversary of this traditional New Year's celebration.

With the war over and the lights back on, a new generation of spectaculars would emerge. The valuable ad space above the International Casino (C) formerly occupied by Wrigley's enormous fish tank would soon be filled with a new iconic spectacular featuring a pair of controversial fifty-foot-tall nude sculptures.

1945

While the lighting restrictions during wartime had dampened the mood in Times Square, the limitations – and the creativity they inspired – helped launch the career of an ambitious young billboard designer from Alabama who went on to create Times Square's most memorable billboards. Arriving in 1929 with nine dollars in his pocket, Douglas Leigh would amass a small fortune from his billboard designs – eventually enough to purchase One Times Square itself. Leigh's billboards made playful use of unexpected elements, like bubbles that floated out of a giant box of detergent, or steam for hot coffee and smoke from cigarettes. His most famous ad, created for Camel cigarettes, featured a changing cast of characters who blew smoke rings over the square from 1941 through 1966 – a full quarter of a century.

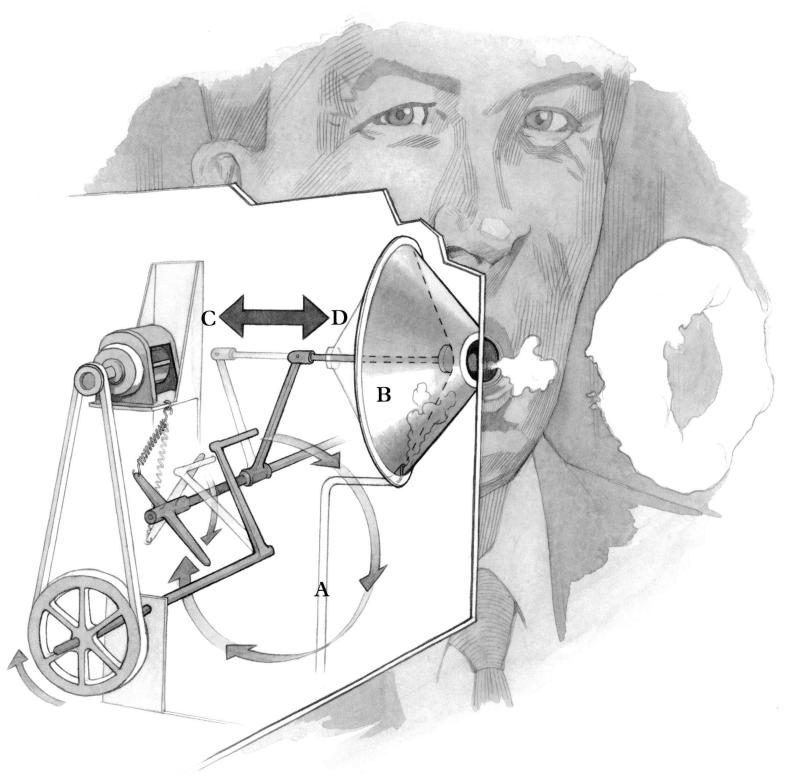

The "smoke" that the billboard produced was actually steam channeled up to the billboard (A) from Con Edison's underground utility pipes. A cone-shaped reservoir (B) slowly filled with steam as its canvas diaphragm was pulled back by a series of levers powered by an electric motor. As a metal rod pulled back the diaphragm to its farthest point (C), steam completely filled the canvas cone. A spring forced the metal rod to snap forward sharply (D), pushing the diaphragm into the cone and forcing the steam out of the mouth in the form of smoke rings.

The lights that returned to Times Square after the war did so in dramatic fashion, drawing visitors who came solely to admire the free show that began at dusk as the billboards came to life. The billboard over the Bond clothing store featured a 50,000-gallon waterfall measuring 27 feet tall that was spiked with anti-freeze in the winter to prevent icing. When prudish guests at the Astor Hotel (which faced the billboard) complained about the nudity of the two towering statues that flanked the waterfall, neon tubes were added to "clothe" the figures at night.

Fantastic neon signs flickered on all sides of the square in animated sequences that made words emerge by lighting up one letter at a time against fields of changing colors and flickering borders. More elaborate billboards featured "moving" figures and objects, among them the Budweiser billboard on 49th street. It used six overlays of neon tubing – each revealing an eagle with a slightly different wing position – lit in rapid succession to make it look like the eagle was flying. The beloved trademark team of horses at the bottom of the billboard appeared to pull a wagon using the same overlay method.

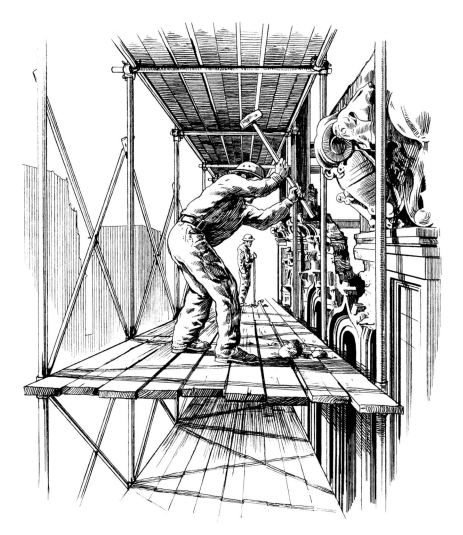

On December 31, 1954, crews prepared for the fiftieth anniversary of the traditional Times Square New Year's celebration. The lighted ball, now made of aluminum and much lighter than the old iron-and-wood version, would descend thanks to the careful choreography of a team of six men (two for hoisting and lowering, one to monitor the ball's descent, one to keep time with a stopwatch, one to keep the electric cable from getting caught, and one to flip the switch that illuminated the numerals as the ball reached the bottom) who practiced their timing to make sure the drop went off without a hitch. But behind the cheery glow of lights, Times Square was beginning to lose its luster. Adult-themed and cheap grind-house movies began to force out struggling legitimate theaters and brought with them an increase in crime, neglect, and low-life entertainment. Even One Times Square was not immune to change. In an effort to modernize the tower, the original carved stone exterior was demolished and unceremoniously dumped in a New Jersey landfill.

Standing naked in broad daylight, the jarring sight of the Times Tower's exposed steel frame (A) prompted one Texas newspaper to print the headline "Strip Show in Times Square" – a reference not only to the construction but to the square's growing nationwide reputation as a place teeming with adult theaters and pornography. The work was undertaken after a change in ownership. Billboard designer Douglas Leigh purchased the building from the *New York Times* in 1961 and immediately hired an artist to render it as a sleek modern tower in hopes of inspiring a new buyer to see the potential of a re-imagined tower. Within two years the Allied Chemical Company did just that, purchasing the tower from Leigh and covering the original frame with white marble panels. Three years later another icon from the square's early days, the Astor Hotel (B) – built in the same years as the Times Tower – would be demolished to make way for the fifty-four-story One Astor Plaza. Keeping an eye on the many changes was George M. Cohan, the influential songwriter, entertainer, and playwright immortalized in a statue erected in 1959 (C). The inscription on its base featured lyrics from one of his most famous songs, "Give My Regards to Broadway."

September 1963

December 1963

October 1964

December 1964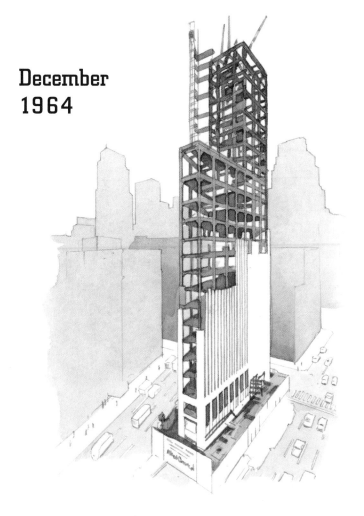

January
1964

June
1964

February
1965

June
1965

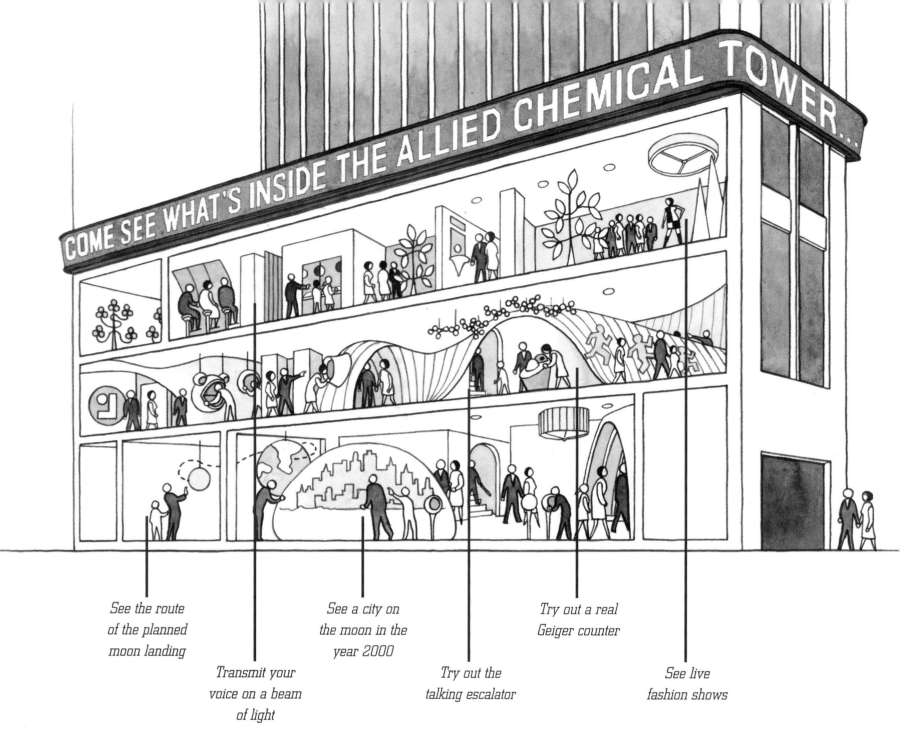

COME SEE WHAT'S INSIDE THE ALLIED CHEMICAL TOWER...

See the route
of the planned
moon landing

Transmit your
voice on a beam
of light

See a city on
the moon in the
year 2000

Try out the
talking escalator

Try out a real
Geiger counter

See live
fashion shows

The mix of tenants who had been renting office space from the *New York Times* moved out to make room for the offices of the Allied Chemical Company, which agreed to continue the tower's longtime tradition of the ball drop as well as its Zipper. The first three floors of the Allied Chemical Tower were dedicated to an exhibit space featuring the company's nylon products – everything from tires to women's apparel – alongside futuristic displays that depicted the planned moon landing (which would happen five years later, in 1969) and an imaginary lunar city called Copernicus as it might appear in the year 2000.

Less than a decade after moving in, Allied Chemical vacated the tower, shut down the exhibit space, and moved operations to a more spacious building two blocks south. Freed of the need to present a corporate image through their building, the owners were willing to sell the façade as ad space to generate revenue. In 1976 the Spectacolor screen was installed on the building's north face. Touted as America's first full-color optical display system, the sign not only flashed advertisements, but also provided weather reports, public art, and public service announcements. The general public could purchase a thirty-second spot for $25, making it a favorite location to post birthday greetings, words of congratulations, and marriage proposals. The exposed nine-story elevator shaft just above the new screen was briefly sold to promote movies, whose titles loomed over the square in giant glowing letters. But the advertisers proved fickle, and after only a brief period of use, the space went unsold as companies balked at associating their brand with a district that had become synonymous with crime, sex, and urban decay.

By the mid-1970s, Times Square had a well-earned reputation as one of the most dangerous neighborhoods in New York City, with steadily increasing rates of violent crime and murder. The grand theaters that had made 42nd Street glamorous in the early 1900s struggled to stay afloat in the teens. Converted to movie houses in the 1920s, they shared the street with freak shows and burlesque by the 1940s, and by the 1960s they were screening adult films and horror movies around the clock.

Hubert's Museum was a 42nd Street institution from the mid-1920s to 1965. A small fee bought access to all kinds of novelty acts, sideshows, freaks, and oddities such as Susi the Elephant Skin Girl, Lady Estelline the Sword Swallower, and Princess Sahloo the voodoo snake dancer. A separate fee was required for the adjacent Heckler's Flea Circus – the last working flea circus in America – where spectators could watch the fleas juggle, play football, and run chariot races.

The subway, instrumental in the growth of Times Square, fell into neglect. As the system's key transfer point, Times Square station was seeing more than 74,000 passengers pass through daily by the early 1980s. Poorly policed, the station's dark passageways, stalked by drug addicts and criminals, were extremely dangerous for unwary commuters, who often fell victim to muggings and crime. A report by the New York City Department of Planning deplored the station's condition, stating, "When the subway system is called 'the most depressing public environment found anywhere,' this station is often cited as evidence."

F ed up with the continuing decline of living conditions in the Square, city officials began planning drastic changes designed to clean up the area. The plans – which included the destruction of some of the area's beloved theaters (A) – sparked fierce debate between preservationists and developers. Steel-and-glass office towers would replace masonry structures like Hotel Claridge (former host of the Camel billboard), which was demolished in 1972 to make room for 1500 Broadway (A), home to ABC studios and *Good Morning America* since 1985. The Spectacolor screen (C), now a permanent fixture on One Times Square and for years the lone screen on the building, would be joined in the coming decades by enough billboards to obscure nearly its entire façade as Times Square slowly shed its seedy reputation while attempting to attract a new generation of advertisers.

1982

Most New Yorkers agreed that change was necessary, but opposing sides disagreed on the best course of action. Plans for the construction of the Marriott Marquis Hotel outraged the theater community, which rallied to preserve the five historic theaters that the hotel developers sought to eliminate. Two weeks of protests, which included marathon readings of plays on an outdoor stage by stars of stage and screen, failed to sway the developer or public officials. In what became known as "The Great Theater Massacre of 1982," heavy machinery tore into the historic theaters, reducing them to rubble. Witnessing the event, Christopher Reeve, star of the *Superman* movies, wished he could transform into his character to "catch the wrecking ball and tear it apart."

Casualties of "The Great Theater Massacre," 1982

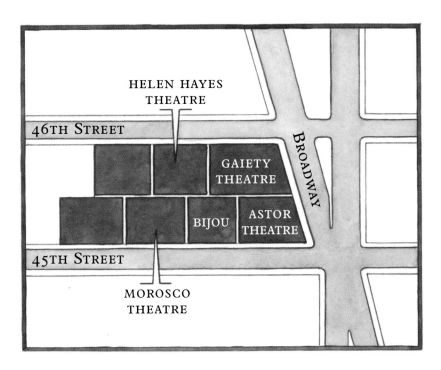

Before

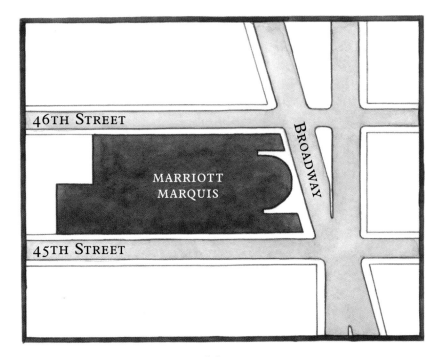

After

At its completion in 1985, the Marriott Marquis boasted the world's tallest hotel atrium, New York's only revolving rooftop restaurant, and the city's largest ballroom, as well as 2,000 guest rooms and a 1,500-seat theater.

For a while it looked as though the wrecking ball that destroyed the theaters might move across the square to 42nd Street and demolish the Times Tower itself, a further manifestation of a massive redevelopment plan designed to drive out the "adult-use" tenants of the run-down theaters and other properties on 42nd Street between Seventh and Eighth avenues. The plan – the 42nd Street Redevelopment Project – called for the construction of four massive office towers designed by Philip Johnson (near left) and John Burgee (far left), but did not include a proposed use for the Times Tower, whose plot was left empty in the architects' model, its fate undefined. Other designers offered imaginative and whimsical proposals for the site. Architect Robert Venturi's proposal featured a "Big Apple" housing a theater with a welcome center at street level.

In 1982, The Municipal Art Society of New York sponsored a design competition to solicit ideas for the Times Tower plot, which generated more playful designs. Architect Frank Lupo's design (right) called for stripping the tower down to its steel base and installing two giant video screens atop the tower that would unfold at night. Architectural illustrator Lee Dunnette envisioned recreating part of the tower's original shell (below left), which would be mounted on the old frame and wrap around an orb with two giant spotlights: one pointing up, and one shining down to the subway platforms below. Paul and Carol Bentel's plan (left) featured performance spaces strewn about the square including one main stage on the Tower plot. The design also included a scaffold that could be used for displaying billboards and a cantilever system for lowering the New Year's ball.

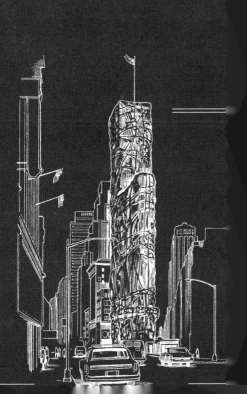

In 1968, the artists Christo and Jeanne-Claude – who would later famously wrap the Reichstag building in Germany, the Pont-Neuf in Paris, and create the "Gates" project in Central Park – proposed their own transformation of One Times Square with a plan to wrap it in fabric and rope. Although a convincing photo-montage rendering gave a sense of what the completed work would look like, the board of directors of the Allied Chemical Corporation ultimately rejected the idea.

In the end, a weak real estate market doomed the Johnson/Burgee project and any proposals to redesign One Times Square. But the tower – outdated, cramped, and in serious need of costly renovations – attracted fewer and fewer tenants. By the early 1990s, the building was more than half vacant. To generate revenue, space on the building's exterior was sold to Japanese advertisers, whose eagerness to seduce American consumers made them willing to associate their brands with Times Square.

After years of stalled plans to improve the Times Square area, real progress finally arrived in the form of the Walt Disney Company, whose restoration of the New Amsterdam Theatre (long ago the home of the Ziegfeld Follies) inspired other companies to invest in the area. Their confidence created a domino effect, and in short order the bright lights that had once defined Times Square began to return as new businesses mounted large signs announcing their presence.

1993   1997

The New Amsterdam Theatre Reborn

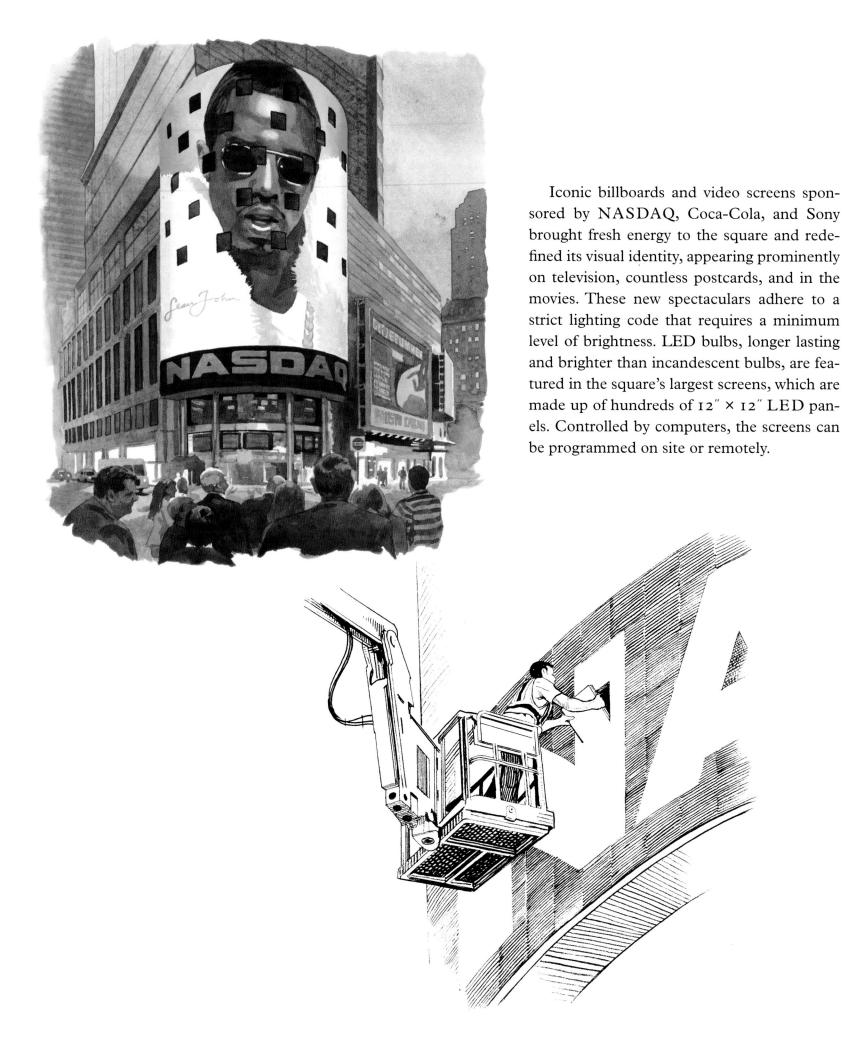

Iconic billboards and video screens sponsored by NASDAQ, Coca-Cola, and Sony brought fresh energy to the square and redefined its visual identity, appearing prominently on television, countless postcards, and in the movies. These new spectaculars adhere to a strict lighting code that requires a minimum level of brightness. LED bulbs, longer lasting and brighter than incandescent bulbs, are featured in the square's largest screens, which are made up of hundreds of 12″ × 12″ LED panels. Controlled by computers, the screens can be programmed on site or remotely.

Among the most widely publicized make-overs was that of the New Year's ball – center-piece of the oldest tradition in the square – which was completely remade in anticipation of the millennial New Year's celebration.

SOME FACTS & FIGURES:

The 2000 "Millenium" ball is 6′0″ in diameter and weighs 1,070 lbs.

The ball is covered with 504 Waterford crystal triangles. These triangles are bolted to 168 translucent triangular clear polycarbonate panels, which are attached to the aluminum frame of the ball.

The exterior of the ball is illuminated by 168 Philips Halogena Brilliant Crystal lightbulbs, exclusively engineered for the New Year's Eve Ball.

The exterior of the ball features 90 rotating pyramid mirrors that reflect light into the audience in Times Square.

¼″ steel support cables and ¼″ steel cable guides stabilize the ball's descent.

The interior of the ball is illuminated by 432 Philips lightbulbs (208 clear, 56 red, 56 blue, 56 green, and 56 yellow) and 96 high-intensity strobe lights.

The 696 lights and 90 rotating pyramid mirrors are computer controlled to produce kaleidoscopic effects atop One Times Square.

The ball descends 77 feet in 60 seconds.

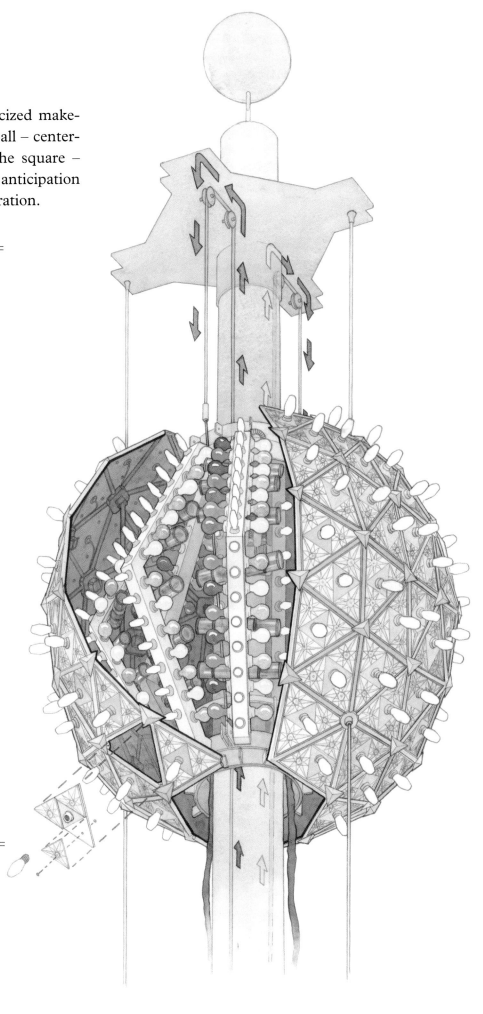

The 1990s brought a building boom to Times Square with the addition of two major skyscrapers: the forty-two-story Bertelsmann Building (A) and the forty-eight-story Condé Nast Building / 4 Times Square (just visible here from the NASDAQ billboard mounted at its northwest corner [B]). The New Year's celebration for the year 2000 (C) was attended by an overflow crowd estimated at two million people, making it the largest celebration in the square since the end of the Second World War. In 2009, lawn chairs and tables were placed on Broadway between 42nd and 47th Streets in an effort by Mayor Michael Bloomberg's office to reduce pedestrian injuries and improve the overall traffic flow of Midtown Manhattan.

2000

Today, One Times Square hosts more than 20 separate billboards, both electronic and vinyl, that generate an estimated $60 million annually, making it the most valuable signpost in the world.

Apart from Walgreen's pharmacy, which occupies the first three floors, the once famous tower is now an empty shell, used primarily to house the computers that run the complex billboards that completely cover its exterior.

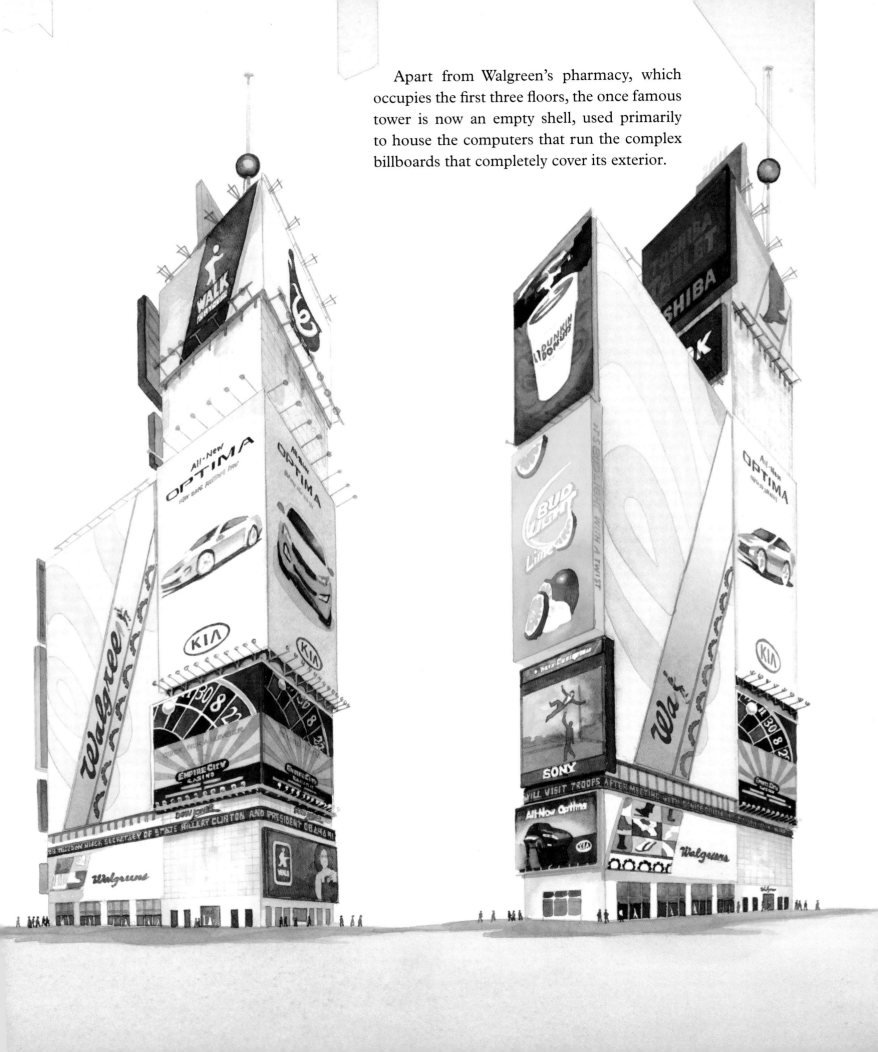

Over one hundred years ago, Oscar Hammerstein wandered through the dusty intersection of Broadway and Seventh Avenue and envisioned a thriving entertainment district. A few years after the construction of Hammerstein's first theater there, *New York Times* owner Adolph Ochs built one of the tallest buildings in the world just a hundred yards to the south. In 1904, the Times Tower gave the intersection a new name and the inhabitants of New York City a new place to gather up-to-the-minute news, follow the ball games, and celebrate the New Year.

Despite the destruction of old buildings and the rise of new ones, Times Square's ability to inspire and adapt has remained intact. As they have since the 1920s, awed visitors continue to gaze skyward at the dizzying array of flashing lights and corporate logos. The modern LED lamps are much brighter than the old incandescent bulbs, but impressive displays of cutting-edge technology on an outsized scale have remained a defining trait of the square.

What changes await the Times Square of the future? Who will come up with the next innovation, build the next icon, or inspire the next major transformation? Will One Times Square survive to host another hundred New Year's Eve celebrations? If the past provides any indication of the future, this five-block stretch of land at the very heart of New York City will remain open to an endless array of possibilities.

2050

Sources

The many sources I consulted as I wrote this book are too numerous to list here, but the following books were invaluable in providing facts and details on the history of Times Square:

Sagalyn, Lynne B. *Times Square Roulette: Remaking the City Icon*. Cambridge, MA: The MIT Press, 2003.

Starr, Tama, and Edward Hayman. *Signs and Wonders: The Spectacular Marketing of America*. New York: Doubleday/Currency, 1998.

Taylor, William R. *Inventing Times Square: Commerce and Culture at the Crossroads of the World*. New York: Russell Sage Foundation, 1991.

Tell, Darcy. *Times Square Spectacular: Lighting Up Broadway*. New York: Smithsonian Books, 2007.

Statistics for the Millennium Ball were provided by Jeffrey Straus of Countdown Entertainment LLC.

Historic and current photographs of Times Square were used as reference in the creation of the illustrations. In most cases, elements from several photographs were combined in a single illustration. Using more than one image allowed me to add cars where they were missing, study a particular building from a different angle, or see the square at a different time of day. Where multiple references were used, every attempt was made in creating a historically accurate scene that represents a particular date and time.

The archives of The Museum of the City of New York and the New-York Historical Society provided many of the photos of the early years of Times Square.

Acknowledgments

This book would not have been possible without the help and support of friends, family, and colleagues.

Special thanks to Carl W. Scarbrough for countless hours of critique, editing, and for his vast and random store of "useless" information that actually frequently turned out to be quite useful!

Thanks also to David Macaulay, the RISD crit crew, Tama Starr and Arthur Boehm at Artkraft-Strauss, Tony Calvano and Nick Bonavita at Landmark Signs, Tobie Cornejo at HLW International, Lynne Sagalyn at Columbia University, Darcy Tell at the Smithsonian, Frank Lupo, Lee Dunnette, Paul and Carol Bentel, Tom Lingner, Maryanne Webb, and especially to my wife Susan for her love and support throughout this project.

A Note on the Type

One Times Square has been set in Plantin, a face cut for Monotype in 1913 under the direction of Frank Hinman Pierpont. Unlike more studious revivals of historic types released during Stanley Morison's tenure at the company, Plantin was freely adapted from the types of the sixteenth-century typographer Robert Granjon, with the goal of creating a face that would be well suited to the demands of modern printing. Such was its success that Plantin ultimately served as a model for Morison's own Times New Roman and was among the earliest types to be adapted for use in offset lithography.

DESIGN & COMPOSITION BY CARL W. SCARBROUGH